ok

quiet

(an erasure of The Book of Disquiet)

R. Keith

ISBN: 978-1-989940-18-1

Dimensionfold Publishing

dimensionfold.com

Cover photo by Niklas Tidbury on Unsplash
https://unsplash.com/@ntidbury

1.

choose

on the fringe of

spaces

improbable

nothing more than

an aggregate of animals, I

a distance

of unconsciousness

disdainer of

our cerebral nerves.

hunch over

the poetry

void

to mould understanding

out loud

2.

detest- ,		my intelligence

loathes;

I choose ;

since I must

dream

.

3.

the stillness

the stillness on the streets

seethe

with sadness

. I slip

verses

until the night , my life feel

of a meaningless lack

consider the essence of

empty

as I scorn

a chant

of twilight

noise in my heart

and none of this means anything

voice-
mishmash

4.

…   the loftiest dreams

in the city

crush me
my

blood

is a bugle

of

pathetic

words

the sunset

stole
pleasures

with

stagnant

jewel of my   disdain.

5.

I slanted

my eyes

Beyond the nothing

rows of

banality –

through the window

like the

blank spaces,

poets of

an unfamiliar cloth,

rhyme is anchor my quiet.

mistake: I write.

this

6.

denied

sunshine

not to feel I exist,

like the spare

-

hearted

unbuttoning

voices,

the patience of

useless

dreams

puts me in my place...

cheap

writing

!...

7.

I imagined

marvellous islands

assaulted my

sense

I end up wearing

lack

right and left

the lure

I prefer
difficult

moments

the urge to give

-

indifference

8.

besides the obstacle

of my life

I'm bound to feel

small

I don't write

now

rabble of

wherever

thinking about things outside

human

crowd.

9.

I understand! - monotonous

Art

never answered.

10.

Everything in me

with itself

restless

conversation

photographic words

I don't recall

I'm

distance-
attached.

11.

We   know

We are abysses-

12.

I

write

with no desire

I say

nothing say .

unimportant.

landscapes

woven

over my hand

...A sharp

reflection that cradles

living

13.

little by little

at the bottom

literature

abyss

I write

woefully

all we know is
our own

impression,

14.

we continue to

be poor,

miserable

I

write,

something worse

but it serves some purpose

for the regret I'll have

tomorrow

...

... curled up on a bench

of my discouragement...

... images

of my life

I crave to be my condition

15.

I was born with.

The swamp

16.

between

my

pleasure

, I lost myself

nailing down

these pages

and forgetting

we're at

a conclusion.

17.

finally

I see myself

emerged from yesterday

18.

smile

passively

my life

over my head

writing is an act

I would trade for

making me look ridiculous

I become

bitterness

of certainty

19.

the cove on

fickleness

To choose

the distance

peacefulness

of ruses…

within

this side of

nothing

drop

the illusion

20.

the circumstances

of
creation
yank
my own hand
from
the noose

21.

not exist, to

22.

I write,

the perfection

fading

23.

falsely,

Let's adopt all the poses

we don't wish to be,

because we're sick

24.

‘So

long,

hope ‘

there’s a difference in

the

unnoticed:

the tramp

jokes

25.

I stare at

the paper's glossy

colour of

a sculpted

sorrow.

a distance

turns out to be more colourful.

the silent shout

of the sleep in

dark fog

to my departure,

subdued

at this absurdity

confronting against

eyes

trembling

where the real

is.

26.

around the bend

voices I don’t
know

27.

thought

Is to conserve

terror.

There's nothing in life

that such-and-such poem

passes on

everything is

tarnished

The

novelist is

with closed eyes

28.

breath of
something that would

not think.

29.

the last drops of

a different song

reverberated in

hopeless

words

echoing

pockets

of my

yearning

looking down

at

a stain.

30.

recognize

weeping

burn with

artificial

affection

dumbly

31.

dull

street lamps

around me

I can’t even feel

my body

fading

amorphously

hazy

images

show my

intermittent

secret

a

swaying of branches

this

reflection of

a dirty sea

engraves itself on my brain

32.

Symphony of less

shapeless

gusts

hushed

my

universal

trap door

33.

I

enjoy
thought not working

I write

on a narrow side

drowsy

hollow

typewriter

of

desolation .

change Art

by losing it-

35.

…

…

…

nightmare,

frivolous

reality

36.

the cracked walls of

poetry

I loathe

37.

object

my

world.

38.

everybody
always seemed

dull

39.

a hand of

blindness

breaks

through

my clearest ideas

after a slumber

scorches everything

40.

to become spiritualized

lacks imagination.

41.

from the sound of rain

my life removes,

into the far distance,

lost in paintings…

a fine dust of

what I was thinking

…

42.

we change clothes-

of the intellect's

dullness
they

are pigs

I write
my

signature on my

tragedy

to applause ,

nothing,

43.

all of the ideas

scatter like ashes

behind us,

44.

so hazy

a street

at rest.

with thoughts

of desire,

stagnation

45.

writing- a life

like a murky pond

...The music of

unknown

burden ...

46.

simple lines

fluttering

to mar with

shout

of empty matter.

shine

47.

… in ray of my fuse …

unfolds

bro-

ken.

48.

To understand

nothing

we've

Solitude

49.

image

slows

linguistically

vanishes

gleams like

anguish in

worrying the night

to learn

of my

species,

50.

lack of sound that

smothers me

bashful

the open field,

quiet

covers!

homesick

photographs,

no flowers for me

in these vast fields
I don’t live here

51.

At empty times like this,

another life

rushes

across

my imagination,

too thick to walk through…

a slow night

closing in,

52.

… voice of a

silence.

sobbing, sobbing

fragments,

…

53.

damage

without illusions

need

our lack of perfection

the common

emptiness.

54.

imposing

end up laughing at
the dreams of ordinary men,

concrete

seductions

made of old, grubby

sound

sip

My empire

Among the

nothing.

I carry

55.

anatomic

author

there's not a

voice

who

I acquire

trophies

of desolation.

56.

a vague

photograph

up against the grimy

familiar faces of

no intelligence

my blank

film

spitting

rubbish

57.

thinking,

the

image is but the

animal squirm of the person

inside of

another

outside my

sleep

Each

thing

I'm writing

the fading of that

colour,

a literary

error

that a sunset is

diminishing

an intellectual mass of

considerations

squished

into my soul,

59.

my ambition

of my life

on a swing

poets

drag past

impossible

verses

surrendered

to believe.

listen and nod their heads.

60.

Should I , answer

.

61.

elevating

ancient

thought

halfway through

This false disdain

the plinth- dirtied by

haughty statue of

no one.

62.

nausea

strolls

slowly

listening to the scraps of

old phrases…

in white paper

drowns

obscenity.

…laughs

tickling

utter

unimportance

the impression

of dreams

leftovers…

63.

catch a glimpse of

big confusion,

these pages

an abyss

searching

a transcendent trick

like closed rooms

I can't

understand a thing...

64.

my weeping

perfection

from writing. Perfection

weeps,

65.

quiet!

pervert.

my words

?

66.

system of life

is a

vague
noise

with
my thoughts,

in my nerves.
I write

soft strokes of

a monotonous
tone of light.

67.

I float.

I don't think.

pathetic

synopsis of civilization

benches were vacant,

to

escape

beauty

is the landscape

in a tragicomedy

68.

the uselessness of

the intellectual

life

philosophies- that

handle their

secretions.

69.

collapse in

my gaze

the pale black colour

my intuition,

And the

chill gnaws

70.

virtue,
novelty

the
rhythm of

human banality,

chatting on

like
marionettes

in a state of slumber

All life is a slumber

no one knows

71.

the classical writers

I loathe

72.

a landscape is

a feeble

finished poem

about

dreaming

rain

the lie of a theory

the solace of being

73.

Everything

around us is

trickery,

forget it.

74.

still
clouds

suspended

cosmically
a kind of

metallic peal

75.

my gift

to separate the idea of

myself

beyond

A sunset

76.

(lit)

an art

chemical

bronzes

analysis

in us a space

of ourselves

our body lives in length

of the
future.

pride in this

objectivity.

77.

no pastime

as others see it

the pleasure I
get

is sad

conclusions

I don’t arouse

respect

78.

bucket

letters

blow

without any point.

Voices

feel

nothing

squeezing

this literary image

on

the outskirts of town-

79.

Faint,

my life!

80.

My hap-

piness is a

paper boat

I can't touch

81.

slow,
sounds in

overcast sounds,

82.

my

understanding.

rubbing

against a sore.

I doubt the arrival of

sleeping.

83.

I inwardly
fashion

this last sentence

I thought
of

Errata

I let

grumble and
clang

vaguely

touches me

I’m a child in

shadows, shadows…

84.

I write?

I wrote

Let's suppose

I exist

in just two
words

a grammatical mistake

85.

I know

ambivalent
incoherent

feelings.

I, spi t

excerpts of

myself-

the absence of words,

86.

Perhaps life is

the bastard

we affirm ourselves.

We livein ba d music.

a dream

of illiterates,

87.

to actually understand

is

a sealed package

all it contains is dust

of a sentence

88.

I want

A lap

to

sleep on

I imagine,

because I can think about it.

the leaves fall

in my desolation

89.

superior man is

useless,

thought

90.

Illusion and
illusion

Anything and everything,

a hindrance

nevertheless

One can sleep

through

yearning

without the intellect

thought

turned inside
out –

better to be

the leech

under the eyes

91.

A glimpse of

Intellectuals

to irritate me, naively

directed at dreaming

the smartest sometimes

is fictitious, write the

novel

write in secret

92.

forgotten

aspire

whatever isn't

poetry

for me

I asked

the distance,

I am still obsessed with

my

imagination

full of problems,

I dream

out loud,

I throw my

nostalgia

over the corpse of

my pseudo-life,

in a make-believe

countryside that never existed

whether or not

I

had a meaning

I've created,

to live and to act

writing

words

through

93.

suffered

the

chambers

since thought

itself

swirling

voice

of longing

94.

tomorrow

shadows

[you]

ships

regret

95.

seashore

aspirations

achieve

their music

with a faint

mistake,

...

up and down the invisible

I feel

beating

nocturnal

96.

see dreamed landscapes

my

dream, I’m
my dream

is

of

dreams had

of
dreams aren’t

of dreams and

of dreams are

97.

The truly wise

covers

realities

98.

my soul the soil

nausea,

impression

sobbing*

false

I saw ashes

I

understand

life's stupidity

dirty brown

fairy tale

to be this way.

99.

set of armour

half-sleep,

in my
stomach,

writing

the empty cup

100.

My will

my own vestige

of the page

where the

stars are again coming out.

101.

standing by the window,

beyond forever!

A slow

restless

wor d

.

102.

sense

has nothing to do with

being.

my dream

turned the corner

out of

my person

a lousy sunset,

103.

cultive a flower

dissenting

104.

general

acceptance

is stupid

105.

all the marks of frustration

like a load of jewels.

106.

from the books

I feel a nausea,

on desire

calling myself
a genius,

trampled on by

my dreams

107.

I don't have any idea

to rest

to think

the smell of ocean

streams

inwardly

108.

to feel life

by proxy

109.

Above

what's really happening

shatters on

the ground

I'll

be no different.

110.

holding the hand of my

sleeping mind

I exist.

111.

the
imagination
thinks it fits

under the fraying

cloth

112.

What we love is the idea

of

our own idea,

fool

as shared words

naked as a skeleton

113.

giving up

experience

this theory

is a complicated jabber

114.

in these

pages

I've sculpted

my self-awarness

to

tamper with

exactly like

a work of art

115.

be closer

without

art

116.

To write is to

retreat

into a slumber

117.

to use the

eyes

in a wire spring

sensation

on the verge of tears

an idiot

in a well-known poet

wiles of our digestion

of the meaningless

118.

I care I write? I
write

I publish

I'd be sorry

I doubt I'd be

I've written

I'm sure

119.

disappointed

fruit

120.

all-too-human

I passively resist

my dreams

never bothered me

121.

organic love

122.

nauseates me.

The stagnation of

someone else

the

horrendous

sensation stuck to another

123.

When I concentrate,

I write

into

abysses

a word

opens up in me

mirrored.

124.

to live life in

a fatigue

to yield

this soul

inadequately and in vain

ambition is no

sphere of

intelligence

it wasn't necessary to live

well

125.

this book

lies in the

void.

126.

I

in my self-misunderstanding

I'm

a for-

eign language.

127.

I don't get
strong; I don't

noble; I don't

And
I'm neither

great. I suffer and I dream I
complain because I'm weak

since I'm an artist, I amuse

beautiful.

I only then I could

then I could

suffering.

I don't world. I don't

universe I'm not pessimist. I suffer
but I don't

do I know

should I care know?

I suffer if I deserve
(doe.)

I'm not pessimist. I'm sad.

128.

I prefer

remaining

to revel

more subtle

129.

the loud voice

started

retreating

My lungs

other

people

heard

heavy pages

130.

writting

is a form of

stupid or crude

denial
and evasion

in the blank space of

-'No thanks'-

131.

nothing to

feel with the mind

wrapping

the absurd tentacle of

Fate

132.

the

function of

thinking

among

shadows

133.

envy prompts

a dunghill of

ourselves

swinging

pendulum

134.

I belong to

selective details

the ornamental

something
of my soul.

135.

my voice gets

squeamish about existing

of silk,

of those who

dreamed

the calm streets

136.

The feeling of having

137.

the
intelligence which

lies

to

me

138.

the narrowest sense,

which we call culture

teaches nothing

reality

is the sunset

I won't have

139.

Unfortunately,

sleeping

behind my work.

my pedestrian's

reflection

forgotten

living

I haven't been

140.

Suicide

by writing about it

literature has no other

ambition

as genuinely

humble

141.

the day's sorrow

squeezes my throat

142.

I plum-

met, between

the quiet

143.

lulling

with our normal life

I can't be a part of

what isn't dreaming

144.

I have nothing
I feel old
every minute
brings back

puddles
dirty

dreaming

I can
have pleasure of

watching

the ordi-nary world
slumber

my
only good suit,

remembers and weeps

of noisy silences

and what I've
lost

145.

the more complete; and the more complete,

These thoughts occurred to me

As I laid the paper down

in the back corner

commensurate with   stature

there isn't even a difference
in

no one

in the corner

I've always felt that virtue lies

It may be illusory,

poems   write

that the future

thought of   this very page

could
bring me fame

and inwardly majes-tic

reflections

146.

a great dream in life that they

have no dream

147.

I struggle

a certain way

the intention of

human culture

148.

the perfection
of

the perfection of

the perfection of

the difference

149.

from, 'Man is or 'Man is
what. 'Man is
true. 'Man is

in the
formative stage

The Greek Anthology

is no more than child's play

writing
that

distance between

the distance between
forgotten phrase

we're shadows of
gestures

Hercules and a
riddle

autonomous shadows, the poetry of

going to sleep

150.

disguising

without knowing

we live
in an illusion

-like so many pretty objects.

everyone who utters such a
phrase is

pork chops

take the
rottenness

about their involuntary pleasures

just as a common corpse is
lowered

151.

in the slow

fluttering shadows

I

so

exist

like

lonely air

In the

depths of

heavy

threads

152.

I achieve

the
courage

of
silently collapsing

I write, if can't write any
didn't write what

the
struggle
to write is

the ruins of

echoing the
soul
To write is
lost

153.

my effort

154.

to myself

wearies

155.

people

have nothing to

dream

the

emptiness

of

sleep

I linger over

In

writing

the sheet of

paper was blank

Extinguished

memory

dropped from

limp fingers

156.

the pageboy of

my
soul dropped in the

water

157.

I'm still far from realizing

power of

pleasure to

create

metaphors

tucked away

in the shadows...

learning to dream

the human

falsehood

No matter.

a figure in a painting

going hungry

158.

ravashed

dreams

flat

159.

From my present vantage point

Nothing happened

imagination (
)

can't

cheat on us

160.

scattered and dull clouds

filled

my intelligence

beyond repair

write a
fluent

thought

of

colourless

stale words

greyly lathering the
sky

161.

the

vocabulary

is unpleasant to me

make-believe

gift of speech

glittering

ills

humanity as merely

painting

between

unfeeling

breeze

162.

we make fools of

our soul

our enemy

the image is absurd

we pretend

we're ourselves

nothing to

crumble

163.

imagination risks

involuntary

slaves of

life

164.

Inaction

is the throne

165.

decoration

is living

more beautiful

in the distance

of animated idiots

166.

to sleep

to sleep

167.

like being led into

a set of

indecipherable fog

I want to stop seeing

168.

... life,

as

gross horror

169.

Page by page

in these idle moments

reclusive living syllable

my prose

insults

life

170.

I exist

simply to get

the compulsion to

pass on

171.

the monotony of

regret

has been in

more often

the

literary imagination

must

do

others well

the greatest book

is basically

monotony

existence

of a modest

apocalypse

of novelty

of true wisdom

Making daily life

visions of me escaping

Because I'm

able to imagine

172.

autumn

clouds smother

me

173.

the worst of drugs

is

who I am

174.

I've dragged my feet through

sleep

shut off from

all around me

I'm more myself

when

I

delude

against

the

world's existence

175.

My generation

couldn't find any support

in the moral sphere

the midst of

metaphysical problems

called "positivism"

all rules of life

clash

over

cultural foundations

of its own

innovations

Today the wor d belongs only to the stupid

176.

                    halfway between

reason

                    there's some-

thing understandable

177.

therories

can fool us

in

pleasure

shackled to

the

kindness, indifferent

178.

the slumber

we really are

in our eyes

exists

poetic

supposedly

life, is

an excited shadow

179.

guide us

a speck of dust

180.

I

hardly write

pleasure

better pleasure loses its lustre

I'll find another

sense

full of idiotic

sorrows

181.

my
imagination
skim,
without reading

skimmed in my soul

various silk figures passing by,
passing by

like slobber

182.

I'm something

if I seek myself

My boredom with

my soul

gave me

being

the clouds slowly

creeping

We sweated

shadows of

depressing

windows

184.

glory

makes

nostalgia nothing

I'm

lost

And

all dissolved to

the last coloured clouds

of horror

I'm a shelf of empty jars.

185.

May this shrink to

dawn

where I belong

with my

memory

186.

night
weaving

life in me
disturbs.

187.

the clarity

isolates

worn-out

days

drama consisting of

disgrace

188.

ordinary

thinking

-that is how most people live

to

decompse

the

soul

189.

a dirty

grey

sadness

190.

the spirit

a

feeling like regret

the usual predestrians

free from having to feel

191.

the sentences I write

already died long ago

my literary conterpart in

which I write

reflecting off

another

begger

mirrored in

the buildings

shimmering

embittered

monotony

192.

straight days of

stillness

weighed down by

The empty
oblivion

...

193.

flowers

disintegrated below

mapping out

hope

impossible

prose I

write

like a rag doll

watching himself die

put into words

caught in my dry throat

194.

I don't know
what kind of nostalgia I

like ....

195.

I've wept

time and

novels

ridiculous

196.

nostalgia for

regret over

existance

create painful landscape

glistening

wide

criss-crossing

a sketchy notion of

mere shadows of

thoughts

finding a substitute for

a generic distaste for

language

197.

whatever

I leave behind

shivers

198.

my retreat from

some part of

memory

returns to

sensation of childhood

technique

of inward

distance

from some novel

made of

slow panting

199.

the pride of isolation

cultivated

too much importance to

reality

200.

a hearthstone

into lofty poetry

laughing fools

the universe we are given

I'm not impressed

or stupid

I prefer a

blindness in

my

nauseated

truth

201.

fog

shifting

towards

the blurry mask

awakening a city

murky

glorious morning

realities

202.

discolouring

apprehension

effort, a vague slumber

yellow of fallen leaves

there is a hint

of the wind sounding different

there's no voice but in

rubbish of stars

strewn over

papers

crumbled into

the

philosophies

ivented for sport

203.

grief just an illusion

swoon

into stars

abandoned

name

blown over the roads

from my sluggish

daydream

scattered and naked

waiting for the purring wind

...I exist without

what life has made of me

such discomfort

my life in

writing

which is

sick of myself

205.

exhausted purples

who I've been

tracks left in

the shade

hope in the

false voyage

I have

206.

my lost childhood

emerged from
the

faint sound of a whip

207.

we consider

sleepwalking

the fashion of

fiction

perfect

mirrors

into a stagnation of

details

produce an

inner rhythm

208.

morality

is

a sick friend

This nausea is almost

literary.

209.

the satanic

seems

to exist

receiving

the writen word

To write is to objectify

the 'real'

210.

the clear age of
thinking

into the image

of

the inactive

211.

a vulgarity

above all else

if we're sincere about
tomorrow

212.

all that we want

prevades us

We dream of

what we have

213.

I was someone different,

I thought

In the clutter of my literary drawers

I've now awoken

pages

of my adolescence that

discredits and

disturbs me

I'm that

language

of

myself

yesterday

...

214.

I found pages

I should have

lost

a certain kind of intelligence

writing

phrases belong to another

I

I don't recognize

215.

I embody

my mouth

an

incompetence

to exist

I want

a sensual nightmare

216.

through

the noisy city

breathes

a coldness

hovering above

with its sad smile of whole truth

city of empty tombs

217.

our

inner life of

large worries

we all aspire to

ellipsis

218.

I seek

the seasons

passing

with me .....

219.

through the city's

dream among

gaslight

sensation

hallow

my detached spirit

unintelligible

Verbal scratches

which I comtemplate

wanting to scream

vainly

220.

is dreaming

of myself

spiritualized

221.

the right

words were

dreaming

myself

an independant nation

so I fashion myself

a false stage

of my

mental experience

a grandiose

palate

of my nostalgia

222.

a storm is

a

detatched voice ...

of metallic light

The noise diminishes

farewell

subsided

and splintered

inside

thought

223.

...

for two straight days

at the window

no reason to feel

shelter

a phonograph

frantically

topsy-turvy

225.

see, beyond the

sunless western sky

there's a cowering mass of

distant

sorrow

as if it were opium in

the cold air

a livid white

loudly hushes

when I'm bursting

confused

reflection in

rugged

yellowing

226.

walking

within my
soul

structural

joy

227.

poetry an art form

I'm incapable of

belongs to

a shadow

consider poetry to be

mechanisms of

a formal body

which the sculptor has

obviously something infantile

the arts

strips off its clothing

228.

Everything
          of classical authors, who

never speak

229.

To read is to

distractedly

contempt life

230.

art is the

attempt

through

other times

the leftover

work of art

231.

writing

torture and humiliation

I write now

I write in the future

I keep writing because

flawed and uncertain

232.

literature

offering us

all

places

by denying life

in

favour of the imagination

the reader of novels

renounce what I don't have

233.

...   sadness   dwells

234.

We can die

amused

235.

love or affection
I've never had the patience
apathy
enough

as a weakness of

my
dealings with

circumstances

a
grand prize
avoid being human

an uncomfortable feeling
was composed

I needed the
monotony of

humiliation

heaped attention on me

my lack of

personification
my intellect

a novel
I read halfway through

I'm sorry

bring me another

236.

an idea

of

inner

life

is

pride in

extasy

Let us stroll

without

happiness

237.

... One day I laid my hands on some

matchboxes

I imagined

my schoolmates

238.

people

deserve nothing

239.

whatever is being

arued

is

temporarily

intrution

240.

rained

cold monotony

of

disillusion

jostling

another voice

enveloping

what

objects my insomnia

241.

The

smudged

sounds disconnectedly

as if

still heat

The atmospher

fragmented

242.

those

abominations

confess

grimy bubbles

lifeless

snot

243.

photograph

the

soul's passivity

the debris

cradles

our awareness

to tomorrow

cut short a fizzled

smother

tongues

244.

nothing

put me into

life

sunsets
timidly

down

245.

the pain

as perfectly normal

of the sad surprise

246.

as accidents

with our eyes

the mischief

247.

in my view a cruel

influence

obstacles

cherished

to leave

home

248.

Abstaining entirely

And thus I'm able...

249.

frustrated aspirations
having failed

a life too miserable
too miserable

was born a literature

where creative forces were
the unreal world

incapable of
glory

250.

I wanted to create .....

true art

with a chain of logic

the crutch of

science

suffers

I can't read

from my own experience

a conscious ghost

251.

tired from

my thoughts

reading and thinking are useless

the frustration

more logical or more

natural

arguments of

inertia

I carved the imaginary

reflection

daily

mental

threatening

nights

feverish

demonic

landscapes

wore

me out

disbelieving

my dreams

dividing myself

dormant

252.

Thinking is a

damp state

253.

... no ...

254.

roaming

violently

dressed up

through a different kind of

social life

or only a
primitive outline of one

again I

make mistakes

isn't benevolent

nonsensical

behind everything

a poet
of

narrow [intelligence]

A toothache

kind of

existence

but it is nevertheless valid

255.

The human soul is

the earth's surface

without

image

only an occasional jerky movement

we live

thanks to

lights and colours

in the philosophy

we keep twirling

256.

people might be

collective hallucinations

257.

Thought can be

mere mass

258.

mistakes

write

dead
poems

259.

wording

doesn't interest me

the speech of others

still shiver

with

pale silks

life's sorrows make

our clear

majectic language

I can no longer read for

trouble

as the

spit

dresses authentic

260.

I supposedly feel

the reader's attention

because I have nothing to do

without writing it

I write

nothing

into real language

the novel

give us

the lie

261.

but sincerely

to love pretending

262.

an unwritten novel

empty

churning

syllables

in the geometry of

existing

demons

laughing inside me

263.

Today

is

a voiceless poetry

in the cellar of

filthy

torments

264.

I know

my stomache

like a thorn

that makes my eyes sore

265.

seducing

imagination

scourges

books

in

myself

(likewise worthless)

266.

the sounds of scales played on a piano

opened

reality

I slowly

reconstruct

a relentlessness

267.

It's the last

moment of any pos-

sibility

268.

my childhood

emerges from

life in the country

which is

literature

269.

life's
already read

270.

Art , the squalor of

sufferings

disillusion

disappoints

There's no waking up

a poem

is to lose

271.

the actual experience

rewards

to lose oneself

ruined

272.

limits

enable us to enjoy

eternities

273.

history

into the dung heap

(a
pilgrimage) of

empty shadows

firmly planted

Happiness

in the solitude

stolen

274.

the masses

losing

me

Those of us in the shade

th geniuses

those whom death forgets

275.

the world begins in

artificial

poets and philosophers

276.

vulgarity

is

sincere

matter

277.

words

with

pity

drool

nothing in life

I stagnated in

a funny joke

like blank

spaces

sad voice

by the whip

Some poets are

pup-

pets

badly dressed and out of shape

278.

life for no reason

complains

humanity keeps on eating

279.

so-called

self-control

stirring thoughts to

dominate

280.

alone

make me

without any

future

281.

nocturnal

shudders

sway

speechless

in the

landscape of

myself

282.

low-lying clouds
    dragging my body

    against the

horizon

        I haven't slept because

            philosophies

283.

If you can't live alone

tragedy

follows you

poor

ridiculous bodies

laughable

I close the shutters of my windows

284.

let us excel in
teaching others

nothing new or beautiful

for

we
died

for our useless
sensations

they

consist of a
wan smile

285.

I live living

intersected

by a strange feel-

ing I exist

to

fantasize

something in

me

I wasn't responsible for

286.

beneath

the night itself

our

voices

entirely

pathless

287.

We worship

paradise

enchant a

plotless novel

288.

constructing

obstacles in

my spirit

grotesque

love in

self-disgust

289.

I would be

a broken

Greek statue

to write

enough

in a single burst

my imagination

can be certain of

a sympathetic ear

in words on

lyric poets

290.

the phrases I'll never
write

unroll in my mind

every word
follows
shadows

the words have
perished

a structural logic
achieved

allegorical

worthless

remains

291.

in art

with
working only

to struggle

292.

My disdain for

all my

suffering is crushed under

the pride of the sun

293.

staring at a book

looking at myself

I stumble

towards

motions that really exist

I plunge into

dust

294.

.....

be envied

295.

To want to die

on the beach

lost

296.

love is

just nonsense

297.

my favourite

believing

decomposes

299.

I imagine myself living

great boredoms

living

them all at the same time

my special talent

of

feeling

my dreams

destroyed

300.

I shuddered

A threatening silence

became clear

ruins in a distant past

with a sullen sound

301.

to feel new without
feeling them

can't feel in

we feel they

to feel new

we feel them

303.

I

suppose everyone is

so vague

the

realities

my tragedy

the useless history

fully write

stretched

the voyage

303.

The world belongs to

the absence of

sensibility

just thought

of

this projection

of

certain

joys

life's

the

chess player

who works in

spite

a sick

deal

I feel sorry for

great poets, great artists,

the one

who thinks

these stage

actors preform the

puppet show

lifeless

304.

Faith is act

305.

a stray comet

of mental

reflections

lurks in

living

306.

I belong
in

disbelief

the impulse

of illusion

enamoured of

hollow

living

any idea

doesn't matter

Living off

the future

fighting spirit

the idiotic

effort

of

simply existing

307.

our mind's

no more than a prison cell

308.

my genius
prettied up

memory

309.

hopeless

ephemeral

speaking

used

a

taste

colourful

into art

merges

pure lines

310.

what

bang

inside me

is a crime

Your silent

gesturs swallow

in

disdainful

rain...

to seek

vice

311.

expecting

nausea

in these moments of

banality

312.

everyone I meet

is a book

words that

disclose

knowledge

shadows of

humiliation

rubbish heaped up

my life

313.

all these people who don't
know

what

true life is

314.

inertia

forgetting

Primitive societies

how to

die of

boredom

intelligent people

suffer

315.

wasting time

with

others

316.

the insults of

soul...

We all harbour

317.

souls

nothing to

me speak with

illustraitions

in novels

brush against

certain images

as flesh and blood

chunks of
meat

bleeding

souls

this moment is bent

a dumb smile

from the

corpse

of
humanity

hard and hazy

318.

...   pass   the night

319.

sunlit things

make-believe

translucent

spiritualized

asleep

sculpted out of

gloom

flowers

yellow with autumn

refection

of imitation

the cascades of

childhood

lacking

320.

dull

autumn

smiling

clouds

of shadow and distance

a dry sound

faded

against

our consciousness

indifferently

absent words of

dust

recalled

autumn

I lost

321.

the song

stowed away

words

breathing rhythms

322.

the imagination

is self-exile

The poem

recorded

in

martyrdom

coolly in the sun

my thinking

to write

shrivel up inside

lulled by

a sail in the distance

...your name that

sounded like

a jumble of

my blood

323.

lightning

loudly

spoken

324.

how to shun

ideas

concrete

325.

Fictions of

sloth

326.

I dream

What kills

what

hurts

the

beauty of

blissful colour

stumbling over

ourselves

327.

If I were

broken

I

would disturb

everything

328.

With your voice and

poems

without youth

unsaid

I hear myself

misunderstand

329.

The words of
shipwrecks

in

words

without the slightest

means

330.

everything is

pleasure of

perversion

Do you know

its own intention?

to waste a life

of art

demolished

Absurdity

of Silence

leaves from

Our

memory

Why am I

writing this book?

331.

a headache

reflect in the spirit

called the brain

I believe

that my soul's

between

two persons

my

stomach

is offended

Sentence by sentence

imagining

on paper

the universe

exists

to make me suffer

332.

my anxiety

I grope

333.

intellectual

something

334.

without thinking

I

recovered myself

stood before

empty

futile life

the slight sounds of

dead wor ds

a

blowfly

shades of

a life

I maybe be nothing

but

Philosophy

without philosophy

335.

pain in the

glowing

pedestrian language

336.

This
sentence

is

underneath me

337.

I feel

the reason to exist

intellectually

grotesque

338.

detachment

on a daily basis

sometimes I lose

my voice

my words

never succeed

on a screen

inside

of me

self-absorbed

with a

language of

endless

fantasy

detached from their walls

339.

waters

abandoned

I see myself as

this image

a sun

behind

my imagination

among rocks where

my slow

surface

floats

I wrote

in another

landscape

340.

in the landscape I don't say

341.

ignoble

words

over slope

avenues of

a sick man

Some scribble

pages

in a stupor of

myself

in a dark

corner

before I existed

in

certain moments

shine

the toothless remains

of

my

horror

342.

I

break

in

images

among phantoms

all tangled

without shape

I'll write

landscapes hazy

moaning

sorrow

in the promenades of

nostalgia

filtering

through

hopes

cutting

cardboard figures

343.

Come down

Come down and place the

wor d

344.

an earth

sterile

and aburd

345.

Why should I

possess a body

there is

nothing

like

my anxieties forgetting

another

humanity

secrets

of.....

other times

stained-glass windows

touch our

useless

existence

346.

one side. We can't

other side. The problem

all sides. The things

347.

in my idea

life

is not

the

moment I want to possess

the affection

won't leave us alone
to read
of a fictional

meaning of this

scenery
an idle

world

dreamed

through
nothing

life

has nothing

to truth

the theatre
I'm
watching

the
clowns

to my novel...

349.

Expressing yourself is

synonymous

with lying

350.

I don't know I don't know
I know

I know

I can't
I think

I
have
I'm younger

I think
I sense
I don't
I
were
I was

I'm visited
I
can't I
wonder

I wonder

I
wonder

I don't

I don't
I feel

351.

echoing

old

distraction

simmering

shadow

still

352.

I see

scrawny

sorrow

between

useless

forgotten

streets

with sudden

nostalgia

A sunset

is gone

353.

disintegrated into shapeless

happiness

vaguely seized by a

reality

when

the shadows

resting

uncertain fog

growing

in spirit

ethereally

lost

354.

an invisible

feel

355.

uneasy

like steel

light

a boom

on a sheet of paper

356.

lulled

tranquillity

hot

laughingly

down the glistening street

souls

more briskly

into my view

discomfort

felt

reality

the voices of the

twine

around

jokes

357.

serious

philosophies taught us

chance

in everything

a novelty

conversation

358.

this wor d

shows signs of

a certain sparkle

garbled

a great poet is

as aburd as

the soul speaks

359.

the

poet

flows

a shapeless

shadow on

understanding

nothing

360.

those who sit around in cafes

don't quite

understand

true geniuses

cutting through

rubbish

361.

The search for

reality

merits

knowledge

of art

362.

Hunger is

the argument

363.

Love is

impossibilty

ours

disapear

we possess

we grasp

flesh

the mouth's

delusion

through the memory

smooth

cutting

I possess I don't

I possess I
don't

I understand
I don't

I know I'm the

I? No.

I possess I

would

365.

the sickness
called

being happy

like a king

in the white clouds

the
sound of

distant seas

the sterile

destiny

The
sound of

my forgetting

there was happy

366.

landscapes

of porcelain

souls

painted

three-dimensional

367.

sickly

luxuriance of

existence

has always struck me

368.

dialogues in

sublime

dead

psychology

painted

fever

of a gesture

the folklore of

True love

emptied

369.

metallic
restless

dream to attract

nothing

individuality,

What joy

it would be

370.

I never know I'm

bored

certain

sensations

clear

nonsensical phrases

it's a pity

to be nostalgic

I can assure you

In spite

I realize

artistic instinct

Do you forgive me?

my pathectic

idea

so true

a plausible

dreamer

distractedly

the sentence

good conversation should be

simply imagined

conversations

that novelists have

To dodge the

rules

how exquisitely

irritating

surely

I wrote

short
interludes

I pretend to be

someone

they will recogize

read

things missing

literature

will

serve as my excuse

371.

I speak

Sometimes

things

illogical

And

inconceivable

372.

I wish

thought itself

shadows

existence

speaking

a real breeze

through

self-abandon

I know

that thinking

set

my

social problem

there are peacock tails

that don't exist

373.

Life is

the mind

where we live

in the corner of the dance hall

with a body

lying in
the grass

the bitterness is

a sensible pain

I'm
exhausted from wor ds

374.

perfection,

the future

storm

the lethargy

tickling

I merely

imagine myself

and laugh

for a moment

375.

we There,

alone

exist

hesitation between

resolved

Miracles

we invent miracles

we can never be

...

376.

bones

in our eyes

I glimpse

sudden

wanting

on the floor

377.

autumn
thoughts

still

pensive

hopes

the slope of
consciousness

violent

sensations

looking down

a varied
landscape

the smoke from

my eyes

378.

infinite

ignorance

cracks

because I think

I don't distinguish

the wor d of dreams

I invent

a

problem

abstaining my
intelligence

for brown paper and
balls of string

379.

I'm tired I'm tired of
nothing

I look

completely

immoral

thinking
makes me

in my
corner
nobody

another poet

copying

380.

I'm unable to

spell

autumn

of useless memory

walls and windows

a wakeful hazy
city

the
image

of wind

381.

a language

is merely boredom

resembles

incomplete

fidget

emptiness causes

the future

the nagging

discomfort of

some

yesterday

its own self

who suffer

The walls

The shackles

the placid

dusk

shapes

unravels

tatters in

desolation

382.

I've

embodied fic-

tion

383.

wor d exists on stage

384.

...   everything is

frustration

.....

385.

like a disease

of the eyes

had taken shape

to
disguise itself

coloured
where it had
stagnated

nothing to do

blurring

in all directions

another wor d

another mind

386.

crackling

the ground

we were two minds

what we

could hear, in

sounds of

no landscape

in an autumn that was

forgotten

trampled leaves

forever

knowing

sadness

Our

steps

had become

foreign

to us

over dead leaves

387.

decadent

glimmers of

unusual

words I think

in the spirit of a

classical writter

the decorative

written

lies

I attempt

in the

words

Beset by

images

diverting me from

long voyages

as soon as I stand up

to abandon myself to the

concrete

388.

the motto I want

in

contamination

I aspire to be

other people's opinions

an ailment

to

perform

movement

390.

To know how to be still

distinguishes the man

391.

my idle

life

is mathematics

the other sciences

don't matter

truth

just

a pile of bricks

remain

without thought

the

first page of

the rain had

their stupid gaze

392.

anarrow focus

of

severing

spells

393.

we live for

sorrows

my inattention

flowing

cries of

motors

shaking

the laughter

exists for me

through

irritation

the anaphrodisiac

I picture

cutting the echo of

the wor d

this inner sunset

without thinking

people live like this

standing still

humanity

is slumber

and the
doorbell rings

394.

at will I dream

with another kind of

regret

395.

The gentle
prayer

silky

mingled with

living

fallaciously

among
the

unshaded

melody

when we glimpse

the clowns

quivering

incomplete
and

dying

benevolent

words

stripped
leaving

the shadows

among

faint wings

all
dead divine

396.

a damp mirror

in our hearts

we're subjects of

disdaining

rain

jotting down these impressions

I'm

writing them

hands still

a single shadow

borrowed

397.

shadow

over the city

itself

is literary

melodic intention

memory of a

moment, to embody.

think about

the city

of myself

The child is

behind my eyes

398.

certain people like me

work against

life

without expecting

anything from it

I need

a stringent from

my misfortune

399.

life is what Diogenes

wanted

poetry

belongs to

the longest

distance

I've always

stood between

the daydream

of

my intelligence

physically sick

400.

where

the
mild

memories

sink into

my
eyes

I can taste

my moments in

my past

aloofness

401.

I

created myself

a poem out of

my innate

aimlessness

the circus

of life

about to burst

its ugly

ghostly noise

402.

my taste for

everyting tasteless

403.

my heart ...

of

unremembered

nostalgia

trickling

memory of mine

at daybreak

your fingers

lost

404.

daydreaming

doesn't hurt

405.

Life unbearable

pointless

distractions

we hardly think
about

a filmsy

detail of speaking and writing

impossible things

ideas

lying in the sunday

destiny

resembles

fiction and hazy

landscape

animated rag-doll

406.

To

be happy you have to know

sleeping

experiencing a happy

moment

is to not exist

exclude one

another

Isolate

completely

407.

a child

beat

my weak hands

jolting

every pore

my mouth   is

my lonliness

408.

The music made

melody

that no one knows

the noise from the city

slowly turning

409.

a great sigh

afforded by the

absenses

people and noise

a feeling of

effortless

sounds

universe

the most plebian

among

false gold

I recognize

leisurely

I'm thinking

about

hanging up

410.

opposite a mirror

people in love lose track of the conversation

as individuals

a normal human being

is

the same words worthy

writings

divided into

jokes

as mere vulgarity

I rent

delusions of

moments

being bored sick

411.

the emotional

vanity

feels

pit

against

itself

412.

the consolation of

lying down

ingrained

systems

of suffering

a pessamist
able to translate

which is unpleasant

the pessamists
shape the world

silence

with all its

genius

whereas happiness is

a

certain

riffraff

observation

413.

dreams

Let us ignore life

with all our senses

empty

chiselling

pure

empty

sentences

and

colours

in their divine

useless silence

414.

we are just shades

dreaming

the wor d

415.

My imaginary wor d

come and go

416.

dialogues

I carry

lull

me

the

questions that I

don't develop

in pictures

realm

an idle

pastime

inner

illustraitions

swirling patterns

the ideas that

literature

sounds

of a

complex painting

curves

grim

417.

I know I read

I've never been
I'm reading

I who I

write

I

always

I always

I've read
I've

read I'm
indebted

I doubt I could

I read

I read

I hear

I hate

I can

I already

I read

I still

I'd sleep

O to

I must

I

I read:

I'm not I feel

I read

I have

419.

life

underscores

vileness

before my eyes

joke

to call

me

so-and-so

a useless therory

with a joke

that's

out of kilter

worst moment

the evening

invent

we close the books
against

us

I write

things that shatter

on somebody's shoulders

dressed up

a new mist

420.

waiting for you

naked

the imagination

melancholy

cover

life

in this cramped room

421.

at the window

the
visible distance

imagined

422.

The moon

forms into
snakes

423.

weapons

pointless

forgotten

left behind

the

tombs

shadows

stroll

424.

in the wor d that can't be explained

425.

a torture

of being famous

426.

an
insignificant event

in the midst of

value

to surpass

the
mystery of

suffocating

sensitivity

life is

writing

being completely misunderstood

I lift my head

and I forget my face

it makes me

almost smile

427.

Remain pure

Learn to disassociate

-that is true nobility

428.

spontaneously

leaving reality

with indifference

self-mastery

To treat our

arrogance

truly alone

sink into

uncouth gestures

Let's internalize

existing

filthy neighbourhoods

429.

my life

as an intruder

was simply the

wrinkle in their brow

devoid
of affection

this attitude in

some obscure

commubicative coldness

strike up

impossible

regret

an orphan

unsatisfied

devoted to

thought

but not

affection

Other people

fall in love

for it to perish

430.

Having

ideas I can never

be sure

of

431.

my enthusiasm

doesn't

belong

432.

my own character

only by indifference

for
insults

433.

in midst

belonging

over the floorboards

the world No one imagined

sheltered me

disguised

their horror or

daily reality

is not ours to

knows

434.

a lifeless

frozen avalanche

435.

clusters of

nacre

436.

I see

the Apocalypse
of

fictitious

personality

of others

I can no
longer

sleep

through

my

imagination

the privileges of

sleeping

sounds

vague

I don't hear it anymore

advancing through the cracks

calling me

the courage

of shadows

in the tall

grass

the tissues of

my imagined bones

amid the dung of oblivion

whose embrace

forgot

437.

I'm quiet

because

my eyes

grimy

I know this

surrounding devoid of sense

I know, I know...

my body

an unfamiliar

country

I see stupid
domestic life

438.

a

yellowed grey

intellectual

439.

I'm writting

the

interrupted city

into oblivion

440.

we

speak the

wor d's illusion

found on maps

of

Lapiz lazuli

441.

I

hazily ascend

to

shades of colours

unknown

in

my window

of isolation

It seems to

make the lamp shine

442.

spells of

intelligence

from random

emotion of losing
balance

I've written

drizzly

empty

silks I don't
know myself

life

poured

out false
colours

of vivid prose

I shipwrecked

so many pages

443.

I don't write

444.

unbearable life

that

ensemble

of sunlight

flits up

almost colourless

445.

a disease of

nothing to do But

pretend

446.

It's the

philosophies

I saw that

was vanity in the words

of

despair

itself

The
poet

speaks of

a slight trace of

point or purpose

and
comes to nothing

447.

all philosophies

are

a massacre

for the most

imaginative

philosophy

strikes me as void

profane

448.

I am today

one wor d

philosophy

I

reject

449.

I'm about to vomit

a rheumatism in

hide tide of scattered light

I'd like to die

today

I'd like, I'd like...

troubles

for being different

...

Amid jokes

450.

like a black

rain

over the atmosphere

filling minds

the fringes of

doubt sat that

swift

common

nightmare

opened wide the windows

with the damp air

half-open

words like a

benediction

451.

I go

from

my body

just like scenery

I imagine

poverty

the end of the wor d

The end of

the wor d

concept of the wor d

452.

various

illustra-

tions of

some

imaginary

privilege

I regret not knowing

a responsible idiot

mispronounced the

glowing

soul

imitating

intelligence

as fattened pigs

453.

I look at life with

A slight daze

a confused mistake

my greatest
ambition

stirring dead ashes

454.

don't worry much about

Reading

What really disturbs

the stupidity

posing

worth

455.

We are but tourists in

the mishaps of

comfort

But fictitious comfort
is enough

456.

I wrote

foresaken lanscapes that
exist

through the varied monotony of

myself

I observe
myself in

what's mine

whatever amounts

to nothing

... I spent my
childhood in

a different
self-abandon

my memories of

vivid

the fiction of

forgetting

457.

the development of mirrors

evolved
the soul

458.

There's a calm joy in

life

from the memory

approaching

it's just stillness

starting to

clear

with each pedestrian

seen stirring in

without thoughts

I see

absurdly

which reality projects

unwittingly

incorporated mist

the milkmen jangle

in the intersections

meanings

have been

imposed on them

the banality

imposes

I see that the mist

quit the sky

I slowly

hesitate

lifelessly

459.

I'd like   to be able to like being

460.

sensibility

shivers and shudders

intelligence

Alone

in

myself for no reason

full of ambition

down the path of no return,

461.

a cloud passes

that's my life

a search

for tranquillity

like mere moss

growing on

bitterness

of being

462.

break off

the sensation of

isolating myself

I still move

through isolation

that brought me to

the horror of

living

I convince myself of

another lost

illusion

the drone of insect swells

in the distance

463.

Peace at last

It's like the moment

I'm also not attracted to

I complete the motions

that I can't identify

the anonymous colour of

External things

I can't

understand

464.

the pages of

Great melancholies

and sober

luxary

absorbed in thought

invisible

cadence written

to remember that

I

also lack the privilege of

no bounds

like the landscape of

dissatisfaction

465.

I'm living

under

some future

sleepiness

that's unable

to sleep

like a stupid

mental twilight

466.

face

of rivers and ponds

looking at himself

poisoned

467.

The word

'face'

looked

in the mirror

I'm just the sick part

like a special tissue

tangled up

with the rest of me

468.

we live

against
our own

particular
personality

I may
be someone's

dull impression

by the imagination

aroused in me annoy-
ance

to a nostalgia for

this wor d

a vast silence emerges

469.

writing To expressing

well-wrought

detachment

470.

too much for

open mouths

471.

Once we're able to see this wor d as an illusion

that happens to us

while we are sleeping

calamities die

before us like

Nothing else...

nothing else... No, nothing
else...

attain the satisfactions of the

rigourus follower

with no initation to

believe in

silent

shadow

imprisioned in

a body

down below

473.

There is some

person

off by themselves

who is

the absolute

noun

We all know that we

desire

474.

pretending
isn't worth the trouble

everything we dream

a new pessimism

475.

laughing about

the boundary of

my

dusty silence

sitting here on a

poor miserable

window

spitting

one thing

tangled in my throat

476.

written

artificial

wrought language

is a nostalgia

in the presence of

costumes

477.

...   distant

nothing

478.

( )

tire

479.

a tumult of
shadows

sleeps in

anxiety
trapped in

desolation

480.

hazy

projections

glimmer

Above

the world's

melody

I feel

myself only in my

sleep

my quiet a river

of abandoned

century

481.

the pleasant sensation of

my memory

flatly answered

all my thoughts   said

nothing

And they were nothing

Tomorrow I too

I am for myself

these streets

of some city

or other.

www.ingramcontent.com/pod-product-compliance
Lightning Source LLC
Chambersburg PA
CBHW062057280426
43673CB00085B/456/J
* 9 7 8 1 9 8 9 9 4 0 1 9 8 *